This book belongs to

....

....

The ground looks empty. Draw the players.

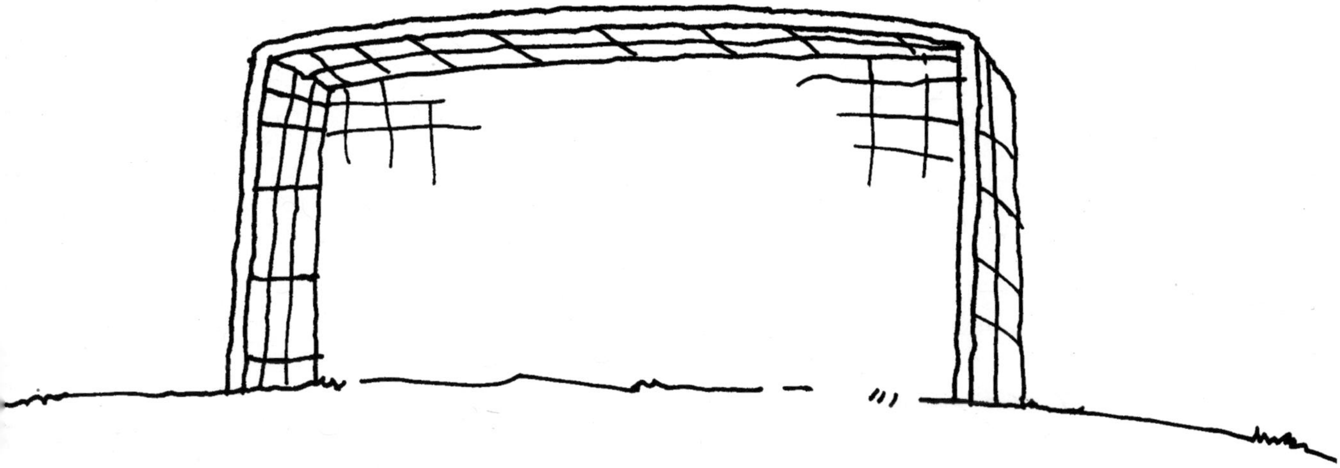

Complete the picture and colour it too.

Playing alone? Where are the others?

Add the mountain slope and the fir trees to this picture.

Complete the picture with your imagination.

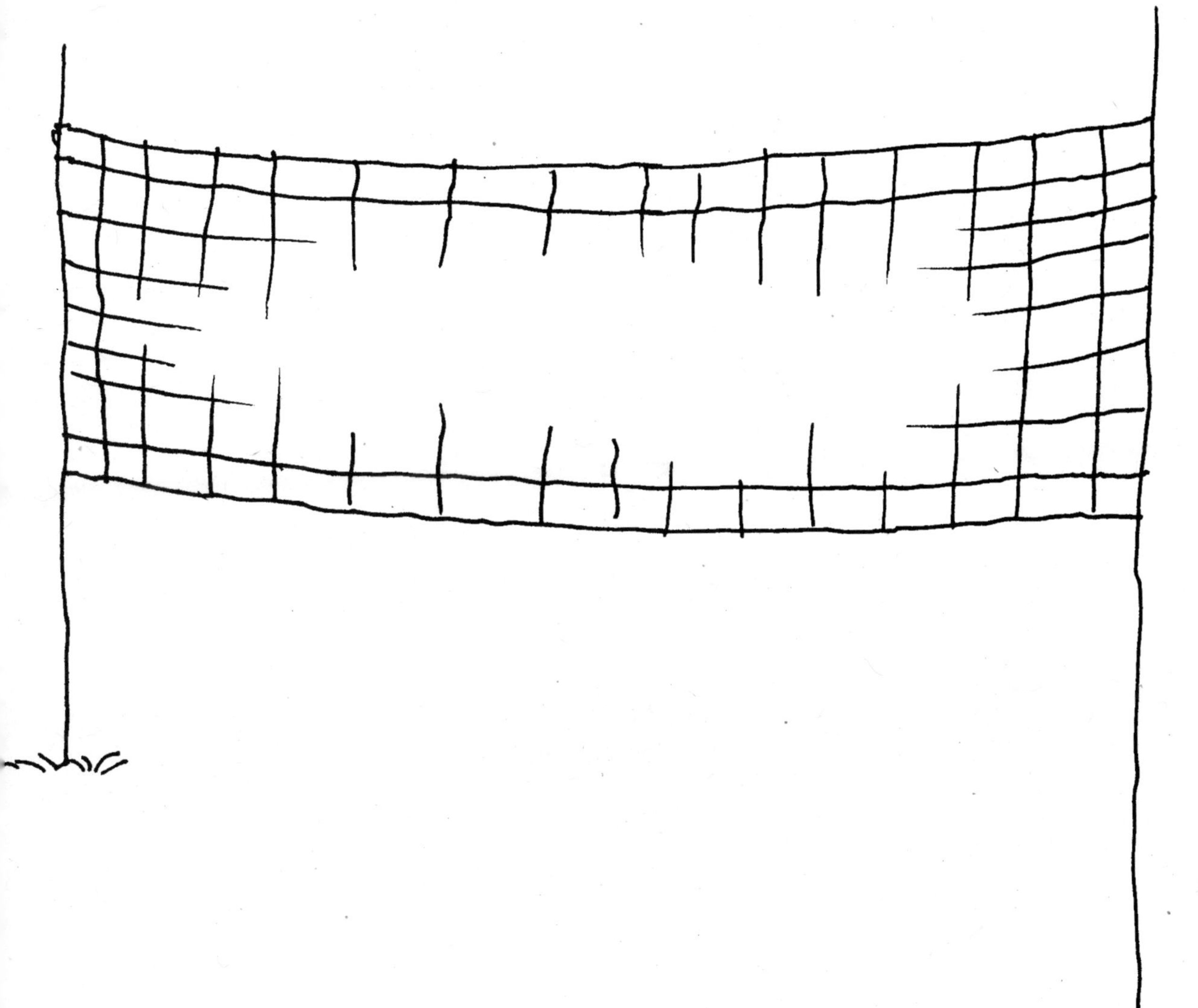

Add things to the picture to show where you are off to?

It's fun sack racing but with friends ofcourse!
So draw them.

Where are you cycling? On the road or in the park?

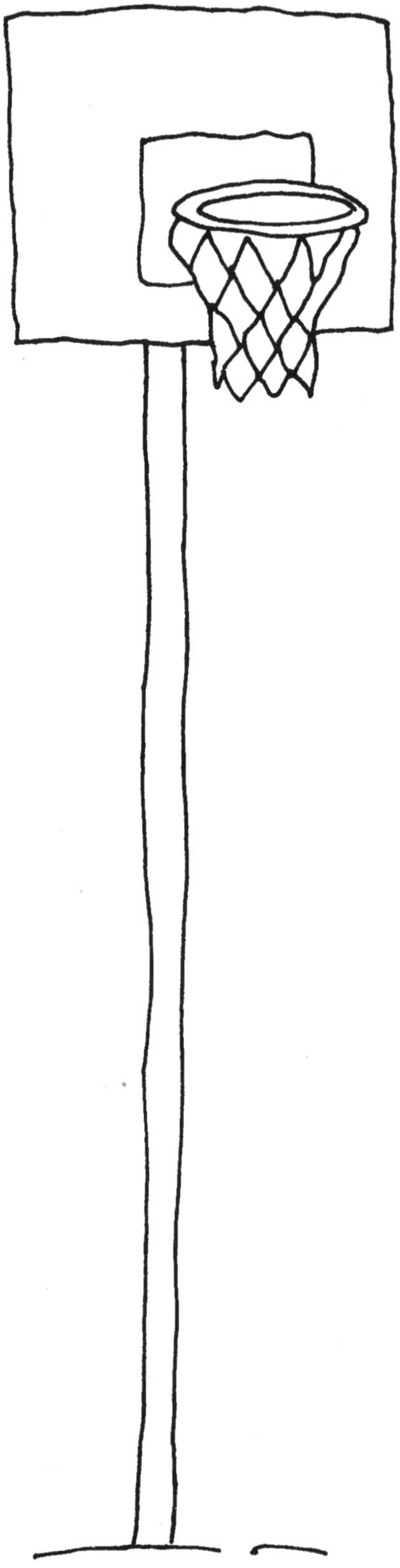

Draw the players and complete the picture.

Draw the teams and the pitch.

Playing hockey alone is boring, isn't it? Draw your friends.

Complete the victory stand by drawing the winners.